Joy

OF EVERY LONGING

Heart

Contents

When God Comes

The activity of God makes the world go around. We see this affirmation throughout our story. In the Genesis story of our beginning, God speaks, and a world teeming with life is created. The Psalms affirm that God provides food for every creature. If God withholds divine breath, everything dies. In the letters of Paul, Jesus is the glue that holds all creation together. In Revelation, the Slaughtered Lamb of God will finally and fully bring creation to completion. While it may seem that the activity of humans dominates the news, enshrines the annals of history, and defines the heroic acts of time, it is actually the activity of God that makes the world go around.

Advent is a wonderful season for remembering this truth. It is an emptying, quieting, focusing season in our Christian story. Into this space, God comes. And when God comes, it is not simply to fill space or occupy time. God is not an object to be pointed out. God is not a mysterious cloud hovering over people and making chills run down their spines. God is not that interested in tickling our religious fancies. So how does God come?

God comes in word and deed. God speaks. God acts. God does. God moves. God saves. God delivers. We know God by what God does. And this action is independent of our religious manipulation, even in spite of it. God is so utterly free that our attempts to lasso the divine for our wishes become ropes of sand. God is so free that our attempts to forge our opinions with God's endorsement are written in disappearing ink. God is so free that our show of religious power is nothing more than a wizard behind a curtain. Advent is not only about God coming; it is also about us remembering our place. Yet God is not exhausted by our lassos, our forgeries, or our magic shows. God still comes. Where meek souls will receive him, still the dear Christ enters in, and that is the hope of Advent—that we might quiet ourselves, know our place, and focus on the activity of God.

Psalms will be most helpful to us in this endeavor. The Psalms name the activity of God on behalf of praying, hopeful people. They declare that God saves in every way that humans need saving. These observations of the saints of the past are gifts of the Spirit for our present.

Each Sunday of Advent has four assigned texts in the Revised Common Lectionary, including one from Psalms, which will be our text each week. Throughout the rest of the week, we will visit the other three texts: one from the Old Testament, one from a Gospel, and one from a New Testament epistle. Each text reflects the activity of the God who comes. The texts are connected. As you move through each week, if you miss a day, go back and read the previous day to make the connections between the different texts. A typical order of themes for the four Sundays of Advent is hope, peace, joy, and love. We will follow in this book an order suggested by the themes of the Psalmic hymns: light, love, joy, and peace.

As you make space this Advent season for the God whose activity makes the world go around, may you encounter this very God in your own heart and life in a way that compels you to go forth into God's good, lovingly created world to proclaim the light, love, joy, and peace of Jesus.

Dan Boone

DECEMBER 3, 2023

SCRIPTURE

PSALM 80

Remember how you brought a young vine from Egypt, cleared out the brambles and briers and planted your very own vineyard? You prepared the good earth, you planted her roots deep; the vineyard filled the land. Your vine soared high and shaded the mountains, even dwarfing the giant cedars. Your vine ranged west to the Sea, east to the River. So why do you no longer protect your vine? Trespassers pick its grapes at will; wild pigs crash through and crush it, and the mice nibble away at what's left. God-of-the-Angel-Armies, turn our way! Take a good look at what's happened and attend to this vine. Care for what you once tenderly planted—the vine you raised from a shoot.

GOD, God-of-the-Angel-Armies, come back! Smile your blessing smile: That will be our salvation.

—Psalm 80:8–15, 19 (MSG)

Psalm 80 is a communal lament of the people of God. These type of prayers were often used in the context of national trauma. A broken and humbled people cried out to God for divine action on their behalf. Christians have learned to pray these prayers following our own collective experiences of anguish: when public figures have been assassinated, when wars have been declared, when acts of terror have been carried out, when pandemics have ravaged the population, and on and on. Each new year brings fresh events for which lament psalms are appropriate.

In this psalm God is described as shepherd and keeper of the vineyard. These roles portray the activity of a God who cares about what is in his keeping. Our place as sheep and grapes does not suggest we have it within ourselves to do a lot about the situations facing us. Whether fighting off wolves or pruning our branches, we are helpless apart from the action of one who cares.

The one role we do play in this psalm is to remind God that it is high time to get moving. Like hungry children, pounding our fists on the table and demanding supper, we command an appearance from God. Maybe this behavior indicates lack of trust or appropriate humility. Or maybe it indicates a deep belief that there is no one else who cares enough to help. Maybe it is a little of both.

Thankfully, we need not be ashamed because our Bible has 150 songs and psalms that expect and demand action from God. This kind of waiting at the table for God to come is in our genes. Many of these songs wonder aloud if we have done something wrong, something to anger God and warrant the delay. But Psalm 80 does not wonder at our own errors. It boldly declares that the problem is not something we have done but the lack of divine appearance. The events have created space for God to enter, and it is high time God does so! So we wait.

The request expressed in this psalm is "let your face shine" in the NRSVUE and "make your face shine on us" in the NIV. Eugene Peterson translated it in The Message as "smile your blessing smile: *that* will be our salvation." Favor flowing from the face of God in our direction is how our darkness is penetrated by light. God's face shines. God glows upon us. God illuminates the depressing darkness. God chases shadows away.

No wonder Isaiah says that "the people who walked in darkness have seen a great light" (Isaiah 9:2). No wonder the father of John the Baptist, Zechariah, sings, "Because of the tender mercy of our God, the dawn from on high will break upon us, to shine upon those who sit in darkness and in the shadow of death, to guide our feet into the way of peace" (Luke 1:78–79). No wonder, when Saul is confronted on the road to Damascus, it is in the form of a blinding light from heaven (Acts 9:3). When God smiles, things happen.

BLESSING

The LORD bless you and keep you; the LORD make his face to shine upon you and be gracious to you; the LORD lift up his countenance upon you and give you peace.

—Numbers 6:24–26

HYMN FOR THE WEEK

O Come, O Come, Emmanuel (*Sing to the Lord* #163)

O come, O come, Emmanuel,
And ransom captive Israel,
That mourns in lowly exile here
Until the Son of God appear.
Rejoice! Rejoice! Emmanuel
Shall come to thee, O Israel!

QUESTIONS FOR REFLECTION

1. List the national tragedies, challenges, and/or difficult headlines of this past year that have called for a community psalm of lament.

   _____

   _____

   _____

   _____

   _____

   _____

2. If people observe us on a day-to-day basis, do we seem to live more under the smile of God or the frown of God?

   _____

   _____

   _____

   _____

   _____

   _____

   _____

   _____

   _____

3. We often say that someone's smile can brighten up a room. What does this mean? How does the smile of God cause darkness to recede?

_____

_____

_____

_____

_____

_____

_____

_____

_____

4. Name someone whose life is a reflection of the blessing (or smile) of God. Tell them why you think this during the week ahead.

_____

_____

_____

_____

_____

_____

_____

_____

_____

Because You Hid Yourself

DECEMBER 4, 2023

SCRIPTURE

ISAIAH 64:1–9

O that you would tear open the heavens and come down, so that the mountains would quake at your presence—as when fire kindles brushwood and the fire causes water to boil—to make your name known to your adversaries, so that the nations might tremble at your presence! When you did awesome deeds that we did not expect, you came down; the mountains quaked at your presence. From ages past no one has heard, no ear has perceived, no eye has seen any God besides you, who works for those who wait for him. You meet those who gladly do right, those who remember you in your ways. But you

were angry, and we sinned; because you hid yourself
we transgressed.

—Isaiah 64:1-5

This text is similar to yesterday's Psalm 80. It is a community lament, but unlike Psalm 80, we have more historical context for this Isaiah text than we have for the Psalm 80 prayer. In Isaiah 64, the people are exiled from their land. Their homes are far away, their armies nonexistent, their temple in shambles, their language foreign to their neighbors, their king a puppet, their holy days not observed in Babylon. Life is not what it once was, and getting back to the good old days seems impossible.

They have been forcibly removed from their homes and sent to live in a foreign country where they are dependent on unfriendly powers. It is unsurprising they might begin to question the very faith they profess in their lament. They say they believe in a God who makes nations tremble, does awesome deeds, and shakes mountains—but it's easy to wonder how much hope is left in the tank.

While the two scriptures are similar in many ways, there is a major difference between this Isaiah text and Psalm 80. These people know they have sinned. They admit as much (see vv. 5-7). However, there also seems to be some passive aggression in their words: we sinned because you weren't showing up, and we stopped praying because you are playing hide and seek (vv. 5, 7). Isn't it just like us fickle humans to somehow blame God for our own sins and failures?

Then again, maybe we are doing what God expects us to do: uttering our deepest fears about our uncontrollable situation using honest words. God loves aggressive covenant partners who cry out for help. Bold honesty never seems to be penalized in Scripture. Even when our messy blaming and shaming and finger-pointing and God-accusing and rationalizing and excuse-making show up in our prayers, God still comes. The hidden face of God is not the end of hope. It is the space between where we are and what God will do. Can we wait in that space for God's face to shine upon us and be gracious to us?

QUESTIONS FOR REFLECTION

1. Has there been a time in your life when God seems to have hidden his face from you? How did you process this absence?

    _____

    _____

    _____

    _____

    _____

2. How is the season of Advent like being an exile in Babylon waiting to go home?

    _____

    _____

    _____

    _____

3. If we consider ourselves to be on a journey toward God as our final resting place, how does not being at home in the world take a toll on our faith?

    _____

    _____

    _____

    _____

The Work of Your Hand

DECEMBER 5, 2023

SCRIPTURE

ISAIAH 64:1–9

We have all become like one who is unclean, and all our righteous deeds are like a filthy cloth. We all fade like a leaf, and our iniquities, like the wind, take us away. There is no one who calls on your name or attempts to take hold of you, for you have hidden your face from us and have delivered us into the hand of our iniquity. Yet, O LORD, you are our Father; we are the clay, and you are our potter; we are all the work of your hand. Do not be exceedingly angry, O LORD, and do not remember iniquity forever. Now consider, we are all your people.

—Isaiah 64:6–9

We're back with our exiled friends in Isaiah 64. Yesterday they were wrangling with the perceived absence of God and suggesting that some of their neglect of spiritual disciplines may be God's fault. At the end of the lament, they have settled into their identity as pottery as their way of reminding God that they are not their own handiwork but his.

Does God need to be reminded that we are the dust of his making, the pottery of his kiln? We seem to do that when we feel like we are forgotten. Remembering we are God-made is essential to our humanity. One of the things that turns us quickly into sub-humans is the idea that we are god-makers rather than God-made. Earlier in Isaiah (chapters 44–46), we make our own gods and expect them to save us. The humor of Isaiah is on full display in 46:1–2. The people are under attack and rush to the temple to save their handmade gods. The gods we create to save us become burdens as we hoist them on our shoulders to protect them from more powerful enemies.

As I observe this generation's college students, I see a burden placed on them by a culture that encourages them to create their own identity. Worldly culture tells them, "You belong to yourself and can define yourself, and you should demand that the world affirm who you say you are." But all the declared identities are merely copies of identities that already exist. As Ecclesiastes 1:9 says, "there is nothing new under the sun"—just a lot of varieties of the same old thing. When we expect the world to applaud us for our declaration of self-made identities, we rarely find the belonging for which our hearts yearn. We become liquid people poured into fixed containers who take the shape of the identities we have surrendered to. It is idolatry all over again: self-made gods that become burdens we have to carry around, defend, and explain.

We become most fully human when we realize that we are God-made and our identity is found in Christ. It is a good thing to confess, even as we wait for the coming of God during Advent, that we are pottery. Then we can say to God along with the exiles, "Now consider, we are all your people."

QUESTIONS FOR REFLECTION

1. Why do we want to be more than pottery?

    _____

    _____

    _____

    _____

    _____

    _____

2. How does waiting for God to come help you clarify who you are?

    _____

    _____

    _____

    _____

    _____

    _____

3. How can seeing others as God's handiwork change the way you relate to them?

    _____

    _____

    _____

    _____

    _____

    _____

    _____

He Is Near

SCRIPTURE

MARK 13:24–37

But in those days, after that suffering, the sun will be darkened, and the moon will not give its light, and the stars will be falling from heaven, and the powers in the heavens will be shaken. Then they will see 'the Son of Man coming in clouds' with great power and glory. Then he will send out the angels and gather the elect from the four winds, from the ends of the earth to the ends of heaven. From the fig tree learn its lesson: as soon as its branch becomes tender and puts forth its leaves, you know that summer is near. So also, when you see these things taking place, you know that he is near, at the very gates. Truly I tell you, this generation will not pass away until all these

*things have taken place. Heaven and earth will pass
away, but my words will not pass away.*
—Mark 13:24–31

It has always been disconcerting to me that Advent texts
are supposed to be getting us ready for Mary, Joseph,
shepherds, and angel choirs—and they go to these apoc-
alyptic, cryptic, end-times, signs-watching texts. To add
insult to injury, the Lectionary suggests a text from the
Gospel of Mark, a Gospel that has no birth narrative and
whose opening does not even pay homage to the holy family. Why are we here? Glad you asked!

Our faith is not limited to the celebration of the child
born in a manger. This child is certainly a joyful reason
to celebrate on December 24 and 25, but our faith is as
forward-looking as it is backward-remembering. Very
few people, even religious people, were looking for the
first coming of Christ. A faithful remnant of people like
Simeon and Anna were hoping to see it before they died,
but most religious folk were getting on with life without
any expectation of divine interruption. Even after Jesus
arrived, most people could not connect the dots to see
Messiah in their midst. They not only failed to anticipate
his coming, but they also didn't recognize him when he
got here.

It is easier to be a Christian who decorates December with
the ornaments of the first coming than it is to be watch-

ing the heavens for signs of his second coming. It takes a trained eye to see the face of God poking through the events of our times, and it takes a hopeful heart to long for a world made right in the way Jesus's return will implement. But even so, the faithful wait and watch.

We do this like our friends in Psalm 80, who believe it is time for God's smile of blessing to shatter the darkness. We do this like our friends in Isaiah 64, who want the potter to come and make everything new. And we do this like the readers of Mark's Gospel, who know that when the fig leaves appear, the figs are not far behind. Advent is about watching as we wait and waiting as we watch. Our waiting and watching are not the main act. God is coming, and when God comes . . .

QUESTIONS FOR REFLECTION

1. Why are we impatient? Does waiting a long time make you more or less confident that whatever you are waiting for will actually happen?

    ----

2. Describe the difference between ornamental faith and hopeful expectation.

    ----

3. How do you connect your present faith to the historic past of Christianity?

Keep Awake

DECEMBER 7, 2023

SCRIPTURE

MARK 13:24–37

But about that day or hour no one knows, neither the angels in heaven nor the Son, but only the Father. Beware, keep alert, for you do not know when the time will come. It is like a man going on a journey, when he leaves home and puts his slaves in charge, each with his work, and commands the doorkeeper to be on the watch. Therefore, keep awake, for you do not know when the master of the house will come, in the evening or at midnight or at cockcrow or at dawn, or else he may find you asleep when he comes suddenly. And what I say to you I say to all: Keep awake.

—Mark 13:32–37

About a century ago, the people of God in the United States recognized the stirrings of moral renewal, and a movement that came to be called the Great Awakening occurred, rousing many to their senses by camp meetings, revival fires, repentance, conviction, and evangelistic zeal. Many Protestant denominations, including my own, were born out of this great movement. In recent years, Christians have begun to think it is time for the world to be morally reawakened yet again from prejudice, hatred, and injustice.

The careful warning of Mark's Gospel is that Jesus is on the move and is coming again. It behooves us to be prepared for his return. This story of the estate owner being gone on a journey is only complete when he returns to the place he left and to the people carrying on his business while he is gone. But the story can only be pressed so far. For instance, Jesus is not actually gone. His promise is to be with us always, even to the end of the age, and we believe that the Holy Spirit is the Spirit of the resurrected Christ in and among us. We are in Christ, and Christ is in us, so let's not press the story to the point of declaring that Jesus is absent from the church. And we should not begin to think we carry out the work of God without the aid of a very present Christ.

But this story does suggest that drowsiness is a real possibility. Lethargy is a mode of settling for the world as

it is. Complacency is spiritual sloth. I get that way sometimes. I'm guessing you do too. The world lulls us into its
rhythms, and before we know it, we're just passing time.
Some preachers would love to use this text to shame lazy
parishioners who aren't pulling their share of the load in
the church's ministries—but how many times can you rev
the engine of activity and sustain it over the long haul?
Who can live in a spiritual buzz that runs 24/7 at 70 miles
per hour day after day? We all need to sleep.

Maybe this text is more of a gift than a lecture on lethargy. Maybe Mark is saying that the owner is coming and
that knowing this deep in our bones is what gets us up
in the morning with hope and rocks us to sleep at night
with assurance. Maybe keeping awake just means we see
something on the horizon that has the capacity to turn the
whole world right side up. I'd hate to sleep through that!

QUESTIONS FOR REFLECTION

1. Imagine the resurrected Jesus has just walked onto the earth. What happens next?

_____

_____

_____

_____

_____

_____

2. If God's intended dwelling is among us on earth, how will the world be righted?

_____

_____

_____

_____

_____

_____

3. What one thing can you do this week to make sure you are prepared and awake?

_____

_____

_____

_____

_____

_____

By Whom You Were Called

SCRIPTURE

1 CORINTHIANS 1:3–9

Grace to you and peace from God our Father and the Lord Jesus Christ. I give thanks to my God always for you because of the grace of God that has been given you in Christ Jesus, for in every way you have been enriched in him, in speech and knowledge of every kind—just as the testimony of Christ has been strengthened among you—so that you are not lacking in any gift as you wait for the revealing of our Lord Jesus Christ. He will also strengthen you to the end, so that you may be blameless on the day of our Lord Jesus Christ. God is faithful, by whom you were called into the partnership of his Son, Jesus Christ our Lord.

—1 Corinthians 1:3–9

The church at Corinth was a fascinating gathering of people. As first-generation Christians, they all brought baggage with them. It is hard for us to comprehend what a church like this might have looked like. The only people with a clue might be our missionary friends who have experienced sharing the gospel in cultures and places where it is being heard for the first time. In the Corinthian church, in addition to questions about eating meat that had been sacrificed to idols, sexual immorality, and economic privilege, there was an issue of gift hierarchy. The community seemed to think that some spiritual gifts should be more valued than others, which meant that the people who received these gifts were often treated as more important than others.

Paul writes at length about the gift hierarchies at work in the church. The effect was that some felt more or less valued based on who their apostolic father was: Paul, Apollos, or Cephas (1:11–13). Some felt more important because they were among the wise (vv. 18–31). Some assigned value based on their connection to leaders of the church (see 1 Corinthians 3). The issue of gift hierarchy reaches a pinnacle in chapter 12 as Paul addresses the differing gifts the Spirit has given to people. He is trying to say that all gifts are valued and necessary and that they do not establish a pecking order. He explains how the body is knit together with each part having intrinsic value to the whole. No part of the body can say it is more or less valued.

In an interesting way, the opening prayer of 1 Corinthians dismantles the idea of a holy pyramid in the church. It says we have all been given the gift of grace in Christ and that none of us lacks any spiritual gift. It is important that we know this, even as we wait for the coming of our Lord Jesus Christ. As we wait, we will be emboldened so that we will be found blameless on the day of our Lord Jesus Christ. In other words, the return of Jesus will reveal that we all belong, we all are gifted, and we all matter to God. So maybe we can live like that now.

QUESTIONS FOR REFLECTION

1. What makes you feel spiritually inferior to others?

   _____

   _____

   _____

   _____

   _____

   _____

2. In your imagination, do you worry about placement among the saints? Do you see yourself as a gold, silver, bronze, or just-glad-to-compete saint?

   _____

   _____

   _____

   _____

   _____

   _____

3. How can we assure a stronger sense of belonging within the church?

   _____

   _____

   _____

   _____

   _____

   _____

Week's Recap

DECEMBER 9, 2023

This week we have studied four texts. Take a moment and read back through the texts from this past week. What has remained with you from each of the texts? Jot down your thoughts.

Psalm 80

_____

_____

_____

_____

_____

Isaiah 64:1–9

_____

_____

_____

_____

_____

_____

Mark 13:24–37

_____
_____
_____
_____
_____
_____

1 Corinthians 1:3–9

_____
_____
_____
_____
_____
_____

What are the common themes you hear or see in these texts?

_____
_____
_____
_____
_____
_____
_____
_____

CLOSING THOUGHT

The coming of the Lord is imagined as God's face of blessing shining on us. Light comes into the world in the activity of God. As we wait for this coming, we are reminded of our dependency as sheep, as untended vines, as hungry children, and as pottery made of dust. We wait in dark situations beyond our control. The temptation is to impatiently forget that we are God-made humans, and take up the art of idolatry, making our own gods. The creation of these idols occupies us, lulls us into complacency, and eventually makes us lethargic toward the renewing that will occur in the coming of God. We learn to live in the darkness of our culture. If there is no light on the horizon, why bother? The payload of this slumbering life dulls our sense of value among the people of God. After all, others have more gifts and saintlier badges. In our sleep, we stop looking for the light that is peeking in from the future.

The good news is that God's blessing face shines on us, our sin has not deterred God's love for us, our God has made us, and our God will carry us! We are enabled to practice Advent as those who are awake, forward-looking, aware of our giftedness, at work on the master's estate, and belonging to a people not forgotten. Rest well on this night. Tomorrow is the second Sunday of the Advent of our Lord.

DECEMBER 10, 2023

SCRIPTURE

PSALM 85:1-2, 8-13

Steadfast love and faithfulness will meet; righteousness and peace will kiss each other. Faithfulness will spring up from the ground, and righteousness will look down from the sky. The LORD will give what is good, and our land will yield its increase. Righteousness will go before him and will make a path for his steps.

—Psalm 85:10-13

When I talk with young couples about to be married, I try to introduce them to the mystery of God's action in the relationship they are about to enter. In the act of covenanting themselves to one another, God does something the couple cannot do. God reaches into each person and drives a stake into the ground of their being, then runs a rope of covenant twine from that stake to the stake in the other person. Two become one. A sacred bond is established. A covenant is made. The Hebrew word for this is *hesed*, which we often translate as "steadfast love." The definition I use is longer. *Hesed* is the behavior that one person has the right to expect of the other in light of promises that were made. When the couple declares, before the presence of God, that this relationship is for better or worse, richer or poorer, sickness and health, God binds them together by these words. God also *enables* the performance of these words across a lifetime.

Psalm 85 is about *hesed*. The petition at the heart of the psalm is, "show us your steadfast love." Why would they ask this? Because it is exactly what God vowed to do for Abraham and his descendants. It is what God vowed to do when he brought them out of Egypt. It is what God did for them in their recent history: "LORD, you were favorable to your land; you restored the fortunes of Jacob" (v. 1). They recall a time when God was angry with them due to their sin. Now they petition God to revive them, restore them, forgive them, and enable them to rejoice again. At the heart of the petition is the deep belief that something in the heart of God is bound to them in loving, steadfast, restorative faithfulness.

This is the way God loves. Because covenant promises matter, God is angered by our violation of faithfulness to the covenant promises that we have made—but not the kind of anger that is cruel, violent, and destructive. God's anger is love. It is the response of a covenant partner so committed to the relationship that faithless behavior *matters*.

We should be careful when translating this into marriage. Some believe the relationship should continue because of the covenant promises made, regardless of the behavior of either partner. The action of God seems to say different. Several of the minor prophets compose divorce documents justifying God's intent to sever relationship with Israel, his bride. For the relationship to continue, a response is required by the offending partner. God stands always ready to receive repentance and restitution for the behavior that violated the essence of the covenant. In our world, divorce often occurs because there are not two covenant partners who are both willing to bear responsibility for behavior. It is not the example of God to stay in a relationship where covenant is neither practiced nor valued. This distance between covenant partners is what we see playing out in Psalm 85.

Advent is leaning into repentance as we wait for the Lord to show us again the steadfast love promised in the covenant. The people ask to hear what the Lord has to say to them. They open themselves to the penetrating truth that exposes their sin. And they believe that when God comes, relational peace is made possible by God's steadfast love. But this requires responsible covenant partners. Advent is possible because of God's steadfast love. Covenant promises matter to God, and they must matter to us if the relationship is to be as it is described in Psalm 85.

BLESSING

The steadfast love of the Lᴏʀᴅ never ceases, his mercies never come to an end; they are new every morning; great is your faithfulness!

—Lamentations 3:22-23

HYMN FOR THE WEEK

Great Is Thy Faithfulness (*Sing to the Lord* #44)

Great is thy faithfulness, O God, my Father;
There is no shadow of turning with thee.
Thou changest not; thy compassions, they fail not.
As thou hast been thou forever wilt be.
Great is thy faithfulness! Great is thy faithfulness!
Morning by morning new mercies I see.
All I have needed thy hand hath provided.
Great is thy faithfulness, Lord, unto me!

QUESTIONS FOR REFLECTION

1. Recall promises you have made that you feel bound to keep. Why does this matter to you?

   _____

   _____

   _____

   _____

   _____

   _____

   _____

   _____

   _____

   _____

2. Take some time to search your biblical memory for promises that God has made to the people of God.

   _____

   _____

   _____

   _____

   _____

   _____

   _____

   _____

   _____

   _____

3. If you have time, sit with the short book of Hosea and reflect on the nature of the relationship between God and the covenanted people.

_____

_____

_____

_____

_____

_____

_____

_____

4. As we move toward the celebration of the coming of Christ on Christmas Eve, how does repentance prepare the way for you?

_____

_____

_____

_____

_____

_____

_____

_____

_____

He Will Feed His Flock

DECEMBER 11, 2023

SCRIPTURE

ISAIAH 40:1-11

See, the Lord God comes with might, and his arm rules for him; his reward is with him and his recompense before him. He will feed his flock like a shepherd; he will gather the lambs in his arms and carry them in his bosom and gently lead the mother sheep.

—Isaiah 40:10-11

I love little towns with strange names. Perhaps you have been to some of my favorites: Teapot Dome, Michigan (there's also one in Idaho and in Washington!); Soddy Daisy, Tennessee; Oblong, Illinois; Floyds Knobs, Indiana; Eclectic, Alabama; and, finally, a town that could only be found in Texas: Veribest. These are interesting places with interesting names and interesting stories.

I'd like to invite you to come with me to a place where some of us have lived before and some—the younger among us—have only heard of. The name of the town is Yesteryear, USA. In Yesteryear, Christians felt right at home. Our Ten Commandments were on our courthouse walls, and we believed they belonged there. Prayer in public spaces and gatherings was both common and expected. Politicians were expected to profess Christian beliefs. Churches were growing; denominational identities were strong. People attended church multiple times a week, most businesses were closed on Sundays, and it was not odd for employees to ask for time off to attend church.

Have you ever lived in Yesteryear? Do you still live there? My guess is, you've moved—or been moved—to a new place. The name of this new place can be found in the Bible. It's called Exile. In Exile, Christianity is not front and center in society, it doesn't drive lawmaking, and it isn't the leader of cultural norms or changes. In Exile, religious plurality dilutes the dominant Christian narrative so that

Christianity is merely one option among many. In Exile, false religion is given as much credence as true religion. Is this where you live now?

QUESTIONS FOR REFLECTION

1. What saddens you most about the church and the world today?

   _____

   _____

   _____

   _____

   _____

2. How is anger expressed in our church?

   _____

   _____

   _____

   _____

   _____

3. What can Christians learn in exile? How can our churches, our ministries, and our faith thrive in exile in ways that perhaps are not possible when Christians are at the center of privilege in society?

   _____

   _____

   _____

   _____

   _____

   _____

TUESDAY

Comfort My People

SCRIPTURE

ISAIAH 40:1–11

*Comfort, O comfort my people, says your God. Speak tenderly to Jerusalem, and cry to her that she has served her term, that her penalty is paid, that she has received from the L*ORD*'s hand double for all her sins.*

—Isaiah 40:1–2

When the Bible describes life in exile, it uses words that indicate loss, displacement, abandonment, vulnerability, unsettledness, distress, depression, fear. In exile we encounter heavy sighs, tired dreams, wistful looks. In exile we experience cynicism, sarcasm, sourness. Exile is an angry, mean-spirited place—usually because people are afraid. Fear manifests itself in one of two ways: passively and aggressively. Passive fear is resignation, despair, depression. We've fallen and we can't, or won't, get up. Aggressive fear is anger, assault, defensiveness, attack.

I've been noting a lot of anger in our culture in the U.S. lately. It manifests itself in political parties, on the news, at school board meetings, and through lawsuits, consumer complaints, crime, suicide, addiction, aggression, social media posts, and curated commentary outlets where personal bias comes first and integrity second (if at all). And we all swim in these waters, Christians along with everybody else. Anger is seeping into the food supply. So, what do we do? We hope for a movement from God.

In Isaiah 40, we drop in on a strategic heavenly planning session of the divine court where the Sovereign Lord of Israel is making a royal proclamation that is meant to be overheard all the way in Exile. Apparently, God's judgment has served its purpose and come to an end. It is important to remember the sins we have committed, just like the prophets diligently reminded Israel of their sins. We bear responsibility for our covenant-breaking behavior. God's judgment is always fair, loving, and faithful to the covenant. But Isaiah 40 proclaims that judgment has a timeline too, and when it has served its time, God will do something new.

QUESTIONS FOR REFLECTION

1. How is exile affecting your walk with God? What kind of people are we becoming? How is this anger seeping into our souls?

   _____

   _____

   _____

   _____

   _____

2. What kind of sins does the Bible tell us typically bring God's judgment on an entire group of people? Which of these concern you for the people of God today?

   _____

   _____

   _____

   _____

   _____

3. If we listened for the judgment of God on the church, what might we hear?

   _____

   _____

   _____

   _____

   _____

The Glory of the Lord

SCRIPTURE

ISAIAH 40:1–11

A voice cries out: "In the wilderness prepare the way of the Lord, make straight in the desert a highway for our God. Every valley shall be lifted up, and every mountain and hill be made low; the uneven ground shall become level, and the rough places a plain. Then the glory of the Lord shall be revealed, and all flesh shall see it together, for the mouth of the Lord has spoken." A voice says, "Cry out!" And I said, "What shall I cry?" All flesh is grass; their constancy is like the flower of the field. The grass withers; the flower fades, [[when the breath of the Lord blows upon it; surely the people are grass. The grass withers; the flower fades,]] but the word of our God will stand forever. Get you up to a high mountain. O Zion, herald of good news; lift up your voice with strength, O Jerusalem, herald of good news; lift it up, do not fear; say to the cities of Judah, "Here is your God!"

—Isaiah 40:3–9

God decides to build a highway to exile. God is coming to exile. The prophet announces that all will see the glory of the Lord upon this highway of praise. The Old Testament word for glory is *kabod*. The word means "heavy," "weighty"—significant enough to make an imprint. God's presence is thick—*kabod*. Israel has experienced this weighty presence in the movement of God at the Red Sea, in the wilderness cloud and pillar of fire, in the Holy of Holies, in the cloud on top of Mount Sinai, on Moses's face, and in the Jerusalem temple. This presence is missing in exile. But now the glory of God is coming to exile via a long, flat, straight, wide, level highway that is substantial enough to withstand the weight of divine *kabod* (glory). And all will see it.

Dare we believe that God's glory is coming to exile? Yes! But we need the help of a preacher—which is exactly what God has in mind in Isaiah. People are fickle, faithless, unresponsive, and hard to convince. We wilt like grass in the hot summer and flowers in a drought. *But the word of our God will stand forever.* Our God is present not in temples, handmade statues, military victory, or political overthrow but in *spoken words*. So where do we place our hope? In the visible symbols of worldly culture or in the frail words of God's messengers? We walk by faith in promises that have not yet fully come to fruition.

The covenant-making God of steadfast love is coming to us in glory. Can we see it? Imagine it? Prepare ourselves for it? Our best move is not angry grousing about the Babylonians and what they are doing to us. Our best hope is not rooted in political victories, Supreme Court decisions, economic solutions, or stock market rallies. Our best news is that God is coming to exile in all his weighty glory to do a new thing among us.

QUESTIONS FOR REFLECTION

1. Describe a time when you experienced the heavy
    (*kabod*-like) glory of God.

    _____

    _____

    _____

    _____

    _____

    _____

    _____

2. What divine promise do you lean on?

    _____

    _____

    _____

    _____

    _____

    _____

3. How do the people of God live faithfully in exile?

    _____

    _____

    _____

    _____

    _____

    _____

    _____

THURSDAY

Prepare the Way

DECEMBER 14, 2023

SCRIPTURE

MARK 1:1–8

The beginning of the good news of Jesus Christ. As it is written in the prophet Isaiah, "See, I am sending my messenger ahead of you, who will prepare your way, the voice of one crying out in the wilderness: 'Prepare the way of the Lord; make his paths straight,'" so John the baptizer appeared in the wilderness, proclaiming a baptism of repentance for the forgiveness of sins. And the whole Judean region and all the people of Jerusalem were going out to him and were baptized by him in the River Jordan, confessing their sins.

—Mark 1:1–5

We know that Christmas Eve could not arrive without going through John the Baptist! John is, after all, the child who leapt in Elizabeth's womb upon hearing the voice of Mary. Both John's and Jesus's stories include dumbstruck dads, divine help naming the two boys, mothers keeping secrets, and the role of one boy preparing the way for the other. Yet the beginning of Mark's Gospel doesn't have any of this. It skips Jesus's birth entirely—but it does start with John the Baptizer, and we are immediately connected to the story of exile.

John is the one who will pave the royal highway upon which God will come. John is the one who will recognize the glory of God among us. John is the one who prays Psalm 85, "show us your steadfast love, revive and restore us." And John is the one who takes covenant seriously, calling for faithful obedience. John understands the necessity of repentance for our covenant-breaking behavior. So John becomes the new Isaiah and offers both the announcement of the coming God and the necessity of making our paths straight.

John builds a highway of repentance, and people traverse it to hear John's message. John preaches about sin, but he isn't focused on the sin of gentiles or atheists or nonbelievers or adherents of other religions. John knows it is not the work of the world to prepare the way for the coming of God; instead, it is the responsibility of the people of God.

And John declares that the work begins at the point of our own sin.

Many in the crowd John was preaching to believed that an ancestral link to Abraham was all that was required to be in covenant with God. John made it clear that the axe of God's judgment was aimed at the Abrahamic tree and that, unless they produced fruit in keeping with repentance, the tree would be coming down (see Luke 3). Again we are confronted with God's *hesed*, God's steadfast love. In light of the commitment we have made to serve God, God has a right to expect certain faithful and loving behavior from us. John does an excellent job of reminding God's people of their covenant obligations.

QUESTIONS FOR REFLECTION

1. If John the Baptist preached at your church, what covenant violations might he name?

   _____

   _____

   _____

   _____

   _____

   _____

   _____

   _____

   _____

2. In your own words, connect the dots between the three texts we've studied so far this week: Psalm 85, Isaiah 40, and Mark 1.

   _____

   _____

   _____

   _____

   _____

   _____

   _____

   _____

   _____

   _____

The Patience of Our Lord

DECEMBER 15, 2023

SCRIPTURE

2 PETER 3:8–15a

But do not ignore this one fact, beloved, that with the Lord one day is like a thousand years, and a thousand years are like one day. The Lord is not slow about his promise, as some think of slowness, but is patient with you, not wanting any to perish but all to come to repentance. But the day of the Lord will come like a thief, and then the heavens will pass away with a loud noise, and the elements will be destroyed with fire, and the earth and everything that is done on it will be disclosed. Since all these things are to be destroyed in this way, what sort of persons ought you to be in leading lives of holiness and godliness, waiting for and hastening the coming of the day of God, because of which the heavens will be set ablaze and destroyed and the elements will melt with fire? But, in accordance with his promise, we wait for new heavens and a new earth, where righteousness is at home. Therefore, beloved, while you are waiting for these things, strive to be found by him at peace, without spot or blemish, and regard the patience of our Lord as salvation.

2 Peter 3:8–15a

It seems the older we get, the more we think about the end of all things. For my dad in his nineties who is confident Jesus will return before his death, this means that, as he watches time continually march on, he urgently prays, "Come quickly, Lord Jesus." This is not far from the experience of the first audience of 2 Peter. They believe Christ will return during their lifetime. As they wait, false teachers begin to question the return of Christ. As their friends begin to die, their doubt grows regarding the promise of Christ's return. False teachers plant seeds of doubt, causing a dispirited people to wonder if they are wrong.

Peter's second epistle recognizes the presence of false teachers and refutes their claims while also urging his audience to remember the teaching that formed them. He appeals to the prophets and the apostles as authorized spokespersons and writers of the revelation of God. In 2 Peter 3:4, we find out that one of the main issues Peter writes to address is the false teachers questioning why Jesus has not shown up. Time, they say, just rolls on like it always has without any discernible difference. Peter denies this assertion, reminding his readers that creation began by a word of God. God's Word is our beginning and our ending, the first and the last, the alpha and the omega. What God has done before, God is going to do again.

What feels like a long time for us is not a long time for God. And when it comes to the reason for the apparent delay in Christ's return, there is good news for humanity. God is demonstrating patience, not wanting any to perish but all to have the opportunity to come to repentance. God's delay is merciful, kind, and saving. God longs for the salvation of all God's creatures. But the patience of God does not mean the day of the Lord will not happen. The coming of the Lord is coupled with the reality of final judgment. The metaphor used to describe this judgment is fire. Fire purifies and reveals things for what they are. It also consumes. The deeds of humanity will be exposed to God's fire even as the people of Noah's day were judged by flood.

God's faithful people need not fear the coming judgment. Judgment will eventually come for the unrepentant, and the timing of it will be as unpredictable as the coming of the thief. But the coming of God to judge is a covenant-restoring act of steadfast love. May we prepare well for this coming.

QUESTIONS FOR REFLECTION

1. What kind of future with God makes you long for the return of Christ?

2. The promise of the coming of the Lord occurred centuries ago. What keeps the expectation alive in you? Do you live with an expectation of the second coming, or have you shelved it in your theology for centuries down the road?

3. Recall the story of Jonah and the Ninevites. How is God patient in this Old Testament story when his prophet is ready to rain down fiery judgment?

Week's Recap

This week we have studied four more texts. Take a moment to read back through them. What has remained with you from each of these scriptures? Jot down your thoughts.

Psalm 85:1–2, 8–13

_____

_____

_____

_____

_____

Isaiah 40:1–11

_____

_____

_____

_____

_____

_____

Mark 1:1–8

_____

_____

_____

_____

_____

_____

2 Peter 3:8–15a

_____

_____

_____

_____

_____

_____

What are the common themes you hear or see in these texts? What connects them?

_____

_____

_____

_____

_____

_____

_____

CLOSING THOUGHT

We began the week with the steadfast love of God. God has made promises to us, and we have made commitments to God. We have the right to expect certain behavior of God (and God of us) in light of the promises made.

This week we have visited the people of Psalm 85, who are remembering how God was faithful in the past, believing that God will respond to their repentance, and hoping for restoration of covenant joy.

We lived among the exiles of Isaiah 40 as they overheard God's announcement that their penalty for sin has ended and that God was coming in glory over the holy highway.

We met the highway builder, John the Baptist, in the abbreviated Christmas narrative of Mark's Gospel. The onramp to the highway is ethical fruit in keeping with repentance.

And we ended the week in 2 Peter, dismissing false teachers who try to convince us that God is anything other than patient, merciful, and full of *hesed*.

Our closing prayer remains, "Lord, show us your steadfast love."

THIRD SUNDAY OF ADVENT

DECEMBER 17, 2023

SCRIPTURE

PSALM 126

When the Lord restored the fortunes of Zion, we were like those who dream. Then our mouth was filled with laughter and our tongue with shouts of joy; then it was said among the nations, "The Lord has done great things for them." The Lord has done great things for us, and we rejoiced. Restore our fortunes, O Lord, like the watercourses in the Negeb. May those who sow in tears reap with shouts of joy. Those who go out weeping, bearing the seed for sowing, shall come home with shouts of joy, carrying their sheaves.

—Psalm 126

I remember the rituals of summer youth camp. We would load our church van and begin the journey to Camp Hurley in Mississippi. It was a sacred space where the presence of God was thick, the water tasted like sulfur, the mosquitoes were as big as birds, and we ate bad food all week without complaint. Memories of how God had visited last year stoked our imaginations of what might be this year. So, along the road, we sang choruses. Some were silly, and some were sacred. A memorable journey is marked by singing that binds us together in a common experience that we are hoping for.

In Psalm 126, the people of God are on a journey, and they are singing. More than likely, they are going up to Jerusalem for a holy festival. Psalms 120–134 are a series of psalms called the Songs of Ascent—titled so because they were ascending the mountain of God. There they expected God to meet with them in thick glory. Psalm 126 is the seventh of these psalms. Most are short enough to easily memorize, similar to the youth camp praise choruses.

This particular Psalm of Ascent seems to be hoping for restoration from national calamity. The psalm starts by remembering how God restored their fortunes in the past, and they laughed, were filled with joy, and offered resounding praise. When God comes, it always seems to be another story in a long line of historic visitations. The God who came to Adam and Eve in a garden also came to Abraham under the stars and also came to Moses in a bush and also came to Gideon facing steep odds and also came to the shepherd boy David and also came to Amos with words of prophecy and also came to came to a virgin named Mary—and also comes to us.

The glory of God at youth camp would be hard to sing about were it not for the memories of last year and the year before that. We anticipate the coming of God because it is in keeping with the character of God to come to us in our hard moments. God has a reputation for restoring our fortunes when we have been shattered by the darkness of the world. We live by both memory and hope. This psalm begins in vivid memory and moves immediately to imagine God coming again to restore fortunes. The image is that of planting a crop of hope-seeds, watered by tears of suffering, grown to maturity by God's visitation, and resulting in an abundant harvest of sheaves. The dry ground will blossom again when God comes. But there is planting, suffering, and hoping to be done as we wait for the crop to break forth.

I suppose it was the anticipation of the youth camp that readied us for the experience. And our anticipation was rooted in the memory of prior years. Why should we expect anything different this year? And so, we sang all the way there, loudly, with great joy and deep hope. May we find the well-beaten path to a hopeful future in this joyous season of God's coming.

BLESSING

*For the Mighty One has done great things for me,
and holy is his name.*

—Luke 1:49

HYMN FOR THE WEEK

Walking in the King's Highway
(*Sing to the Lord* #519)

We shall see the desert as the rose,
Walking in the King's highway;
There'll be singing where salvation goes,
Walking in the King's highway.
There's a highway there and a way,
Where sorrow shall flee away;
And the light shines bright as the day,
Walking in the King's highway.

QUESTIONS FOR REFLECTION

1. How are you longing for God to restore the fortunes
    of God's people? What are the losses that only God
    can restore?

    _____

    _____

    _____

    _____

    _____

    _____

    _____

    _____

    _____

    _____

2. What seeds are you planting in hope of a future crop?
    How is this similar to suffering as you wait and work?

    _____

    _____

    _____

    _____

    _____

    _____

    _____

    _____

    _____

3. What Christmas songs can you think of that best express that we are people of both memory and hope?

_____

_____

_____

_____

_____

_____

_____

_____

_____

_____

4. Given the opportunity to share your faith this Advent season, how would you respond if asked the reason for your hope?

_____

_____

_____

_____

_____

_____

_____

_____

_____

To Bring Good News

DECEMBER 18, 2023

SCRIPTURE

ISAIAH 61:1–4, 8–11

The spirit of the Lord God is upon me, because the Lord has anointed me; he has sent me to bring good news to the oppressed, to bind up the brokenhearted, to proclaim liberty to the captives and release to the prisoners, to proclaim the year of the Lord's favor and the day of vengeance of our God, to comfort all who mourn, to provide for those who mourn in Zion—to give them a garland instead of ashes, the oil of gladness instead of mourning, the mantle of praise instead of a faint spirit. They will be called oaks of righteousness, the planting of the Lord, to display his glory. They shall build up the ancient ruins; they shall raise up the former devastations;

they shall repair the ruined cities, the devastations of
many generations.

—*Isaiah 61:1–4*

When we read through Isaiah, it is sometimes hard to tell who is speaking. We have several speakers within the texts. Sometimes God speaks directly. Sometimes we hear from a narrator who moves the story along. Sometimes we hear from a prophetic or priestly character called the Suffering Servant. This one stands among the people and announces the activity of God to them. The servant seems to have one foot in the dark present and one foot in the coming hope of the future. And sometimes the people of God speak out of their own experience.

If you asked me, I'd want the job of the servant who gets to announce emerging joy. I'd like to be filled with the Spirit of God and empowered to leak good news to the oppressed, the brokenhearted, the captives, and the prisoners. I'd love to tell them God's favor and fortune will land squarely on them and that it will look like justice and comfort. The result will be a total makeover. Instead of smeared black ashes, they will wear floral garlands. Instead of mourning frowns, their foreheads will glisten with anointing oil. Instead of dreary wardrobes of faint-heartedness, they will wear cloaks of celebratory praise.

Our culture is well acquainted with before-and-after pictures. Sometimes it is hard to tell that it is the same subject. I've been around a lot of weddings that bring in professional makeup artists and hairdressers for the women. The women who come out of the dressing room look different than the ones who walked in! There is something about getting professional help that makes people feel brand new. And God knows that many among us need professional help. The exiles of Isaiah certainly did. That's why joy radiates from faces that used to frown. All of this is made possible by a simple announcement that God is on the way to do makeover work.

No wonder Jesus reached for the scroll of Isaiah 61 in his Nazareth hometown synagogue. He read the text to them, sat down, and announced that this scripture was fulfilled by his presence. Read the whole story in Luke 4. The Suffering Servant of God had appeared to offer makeovers to all who were interested. There weren't many takers that day. Maybe it will be different for you today.

QUESTIONS FOR REFLECTION

1. Have you ever had anything good happen to you that changed your appearance and countenance? What might that look like for Christians during Advent?

_____

_____

_____

_____

_____

_____

_____

_____

2. Where is there potential for you to be an announcer of good news this week? What will you say?

_____

_____

_____

_____

_____

_____

_____

_____

_____

Known among the Nations

SCRIPTURE

ISAIAH 61:1–4, 8–11

For I, the LORD, love justice, I hate robbery and wrongdoing; I will faithfully give them their recompense, and I will make an everlasting covenant with them. Their descendants shall be known among the nations and their offspring among the peoples; all who see them shall acknowledge that they are a people whom the LORD has blessed. I will greatly rejoice in the LORD; my whole being shall exult in my God, for he has clothed me with the garments of salvation; he has covered me with the robe of righteousness, as a bridegroom decks himself with a garland and as a bride adorns herself with her jew-

*els. For as the earth brings forth its shoots and as a garden causes what is sown in it to spring up, so the Lord G*ᴏᴅ *will cause righteousness and praise to spring up before all the nations.*

—Isaiah 61:8–11

This scripture offers us the perspectives of a prophet, of God, and of the community to whom the prophecy is giving. Conspicuously absent is a perspective from "the nations"—those who observe what God is doing among the exiles. But the biblical record does seem to show that what the nations think matters to God. Recall the story of Moses in the wilderness, when God was ready to deep-fry the people dancing around a golden calf. He declared he would start all over again with Moses to form a new people. But Moses asked God a simple question: "What will the Egyptians think?" That one simple question seems to be what spared the Israelites the fiery judgment (see Exodus 32).

We are the reputation of God in the world. We are known among the nations as the people of God. God has taken the massive risk of hitching his reputation to our witness. Yes, this is why God is often misunderstood by a wondering world. We don't always represent God accurately. But in Isaiah 61, we are God's glory on display, God's crop in the field, God's grove of oak trees, God's blessed people, God's dressed people, and God's bride. Extending this to the New Testament, we are God's holy temple, the bride of God's Messiah, and the reflection of God's glory that is seen in the face of Christ.

All of these images are marked by joy. Yet Christians today often seem to reflect more of an Oscar the Grouch mentality. It sometimes seems we would prefer to be moral watchdogs rather than harbingers and vessels of joy. It matters what the world thinks of us. God has a reputation to be upheld. The joy of the Lord should be evident in all of God's people—may it be so in us today.

QUESTIONS FOR REFLECTION

1. If the world sees God through the reflection of the average Christian witness, what reputation do you think God has in the world today?

2. Name some people who reflect the character of God in positive ways that, if seen worldwide, would lead the world to trust God.

3. How does your life reflect God to a watching world? Where might a makeover be in order?

In All Circumstances

DECEMBER 20, 2023

SCRIPTURE

1 THESSALONIANS 5:16–24

Rejoice always, pray without ceasing, give thanks in all circumstances, for this is the will of God in Christ Jesus for you. Do not quench the Spirit. Do not despise prophecies, but test everything; hold fast to what is good; abstain from every form of evil.

—*1 Thessalonians 5:16–22*

These short, pithy remarks at the conclusion of 1 Thessalonians are written in the context of concerns about the return of the Lord. As the saints who were eyewitnesses of the resurrected Jesus began to die, there was growing concern that something was wrong. They expected the immediate return of the Lord, within at least the first generation. Paul's address to them in 4:13–5:11 may be familiar text as words that are often referenced at graveside services. Paul moves immediately from this explanation to his concluding thoughts beginning in 5:12.

These are some of the heaviest, shortest verses in our Bible. Each verse is packed tightly with an imperative for the people of God regarding ethical living. This passage is about how we are to live as we wait for the return of our Lord. God is coming again, even as we have seen in the past. Similar to our exiled friends in Isaiah 61, it matters how we live while we wait.

At the beginning of the list is the theme for this week of Advent: *rejoice*. Our waiting begins in joyful expectation. We are journeying with our Psalm 126 friends, singing songs of hopeful expectation for the coming of the Lord to restore the fortunes of his people. Pray without ceasing. Never forget the language of the hopeful soul that converses with God. Give thanks *in* all circumstances—not *for* all circumstances but *in* all circumstances. Seeing God at work even while we wait is cause for gratitude. God wills that we rejoice, pray, and give thanks.

As for what we should *not* do? Do not quench the Spirit! The coming of God is like a stream flowing into the desert. Why build a dam to obstruct the flow of grace? Do not despise the words of prophets! The good-news messengers herald the coming. Why dispute them? Abstain from evil and throw your arms around everything good. Why cavort with the very darkness that God is judging by his coming?

Advent is an important practice for us because we tend to lose sight of the coming God. When we wait rightly, our practices are shaped by our expectations. We rejoice, pray, and give thanks. When we forget the God who comes, we dry up, can't recognize good news when we hear it, and fail to discern the line between evil and good. It is good to learn to wait rightly.

QUESTIONS FOR REFLECTION

1. If the Thessalonian church had a hard time waiting for the return of the Lord, how are we doing two thousand years later? Is it something that's on your mind?

    _____

    _____

    _____

    _____

    _____

2. How do we keep these imperatives (rejoice always, pray without ceasing, etc.) from becoming empty and meaningless?

    _____

    _____

    _____

    _____

    _____

3. Why does the command to rejoice top the list of ethical practices of waiting?

    _____

    _____

    _____

    _____

    _____

He Will Do This

DECEMBER 21, 2023

SCRIPTURE

1 THESSALONIANS 5:16–24

May the God of peace himself sanctify you entire-ly, and may your spirit and soul and body be kept sound and blameless at the coming of our Lord Jesus Christ. The one who calls you is faithful, and he will do this.

—1 Thessalonians 5:23–24

The ethical injunctions of this 1 Thessalonians passage are followed by verses 23–24, which are both a prayer and an affirmation of God's power to enable us to keep the imperative commands. It is important to note that the pronoun "you" is plural in these verses. Paul is praying for the entire sanctification of the whole community, while simultaneously praying it for the whole spirit, soul, and body of each individual community member.

I recall a time when I was speaking at a banquet. I was seated at the head table for the meal with the event organizers. The podium was in the middle of the head table. I mistakenly tucked the tablecloth into my pants, thinking it was my dinner napkin. Following a gracious introduction, I rose to move toward the center podium and brought the whole tablecloth with me. As I moved, everyone moved. My actions impacted everyone at the table. We were a linked community.

It is so easy for us to think of our faith in narrow, individualist ways, but it is important for us to understand, as Paul wanted the Thessalonian church to understand, that God does not just sanctify individuals. God sanctifies individuals into a holy temple, a sacred people, a royal priesthood, a family of brothers and sisters. God is creating a people who, by the power of sanctifying grace, will be kept sound and blameless until the return of Christ. We are in this together. We march to Zion singing songs of expectant hope together. We live in exile together with our ears tuned to the announcement of good news. We share a witness together that testifies to the world about the character of God. We wait with joy, prayer, and thanks as we cling to good instead of evil. But we are not left alone to create these communities of vibrant faith. The one who calls us to do it is faithful and will do this work among us.

Waiting in Advent is the practice of being formed into a community of the sanctified who will not be hard to spot at the return of the Lord.

QUESTIONS FOR REFLECTION

1. Is your faith more communal or individual? How does one move from one to the other?

   _____

   _____

   _____

   _____

   _____

   _____

2. Think about sanctification as the activity of God that enables us to live out verses 16–22. How do these verses reflect Jesus?

   _____

   _____

   _____

   _____

   _____

3. What is your prayer for your community this Advent season?

   _____

   _____

   _____

   _____

   _____

   _____

That All Might Believe

DECEMBER 22, 2023

SCRIPTURE

JOHN 1:6–8, 19–28

There was a man sent from God whose name was John. He came as a witness to testify to the light, so that all might believe through him. He himself was not the light, but he came to testify to the light.

—John 1:6-8

Similar to the neighbors of Isaiah's exiles and the pagans of Thessalonica, the religious representatives of John's day wanted to know the same thing: *Who are you, and what are you doing?* They saw something intriguing about John the Baptist and were fascinated by this voice in the wilderness.

John the Gospel writer does not get very far into his story before telling us in simple language that John the Baptizer was sent from God to bear witness to the light that was coming into the world. While he was not that light, he was a divine messenger of that light. His mission? That people would believe his message and recognize the Messiah of God. In this prologue to the Gospel, we the readers are told what the characters to be introduced do not yet know. Once we are clued in on who John is, the inquisitors from religious headquarters arrive and immediately begin asking questions. *Who are you? Are you Elijah? Are you the prophet? Answer us! What do you have to say for yourself? Why are you baptizing?* You get the sense that this question-peppering was not friendly. John apparently gives off vibes that reminded the leaders of Elijah and possibly the expected Messiah. They want to find out if he is operating on false credentials. He quotes from Isaiah 40 as one who is preparing the way for the coming of God. We already know from the prologue that he is God-authorized. The religious leaders are sure he is not.

How do we know, when we don't have the Bible to tell us, which prophets to believe and which to dismiss? This was of concern in yesterday's Thessalonians text as Paul instructed them to discern the work of the Spirit and not despise the words of true prophets. How do we recognize the true light in a world with more prophets than pickup trucks? Whose words are authentic?

Maybe the answer is in John's response. He authenticates himself by placing himself in proper relation to Jesus. He is not the light but is a witness *to* the light. He is not the circus master in the spotlighted center ring but the announcer directing everyone's attention to the one who stands in the light. And he is not worthy to tie the shoe-strings of the one who is the light of the world. I suppose for us, that means we can believe those who keep pointing to Jesus and kneeling at his feet.

QUESTIONS FOR REFLECTION

1. What made the religious leaders suspicious of John the Baptist?

2. Why is it more and more difficult to find messengers whose witness is trustworthy in a world filled with people speaking on behalf of God?

3. If you were asked the same interrogation-like questions that John was asked ("Who are you, and what are you doing here?"), how would you reply?

Week's Recap

This week we have studied four texts. Take a moment and read back through them. What has remained with you from each text? Jot down your thoughts.

Psalm 126

_____

_____

_____

_____

_____

_____

Isaiah 61:1–4, 8–11

_____

_____

_____

_____

_____

_____

1 Thessalonians 5:16–24

_____

_____

_____

_____

_____

John 1:6–8, 19–28

_____

_____

_____

_____

_____

What are the common themes you hear or see in these texts?

_____

_____

_____

_____

_____

_____

_____

CLOSING THOUGHT

We have spent this third week of Advent with the prophets of good news. We began the week with the people of God going up to Jerusalem, singing a Psalm of Ascent. We join them in this journey toward thick glory in hopes that God will restore the fortunes of the faithful.

We then lived with the exiles of Isaiah as we heard the prophet announce the good news that God comes to the oppressed, brokenhearted, and captive, bringing justice and comfort. This startling news is so transforming that it changes our very countenance. The divine makeover turns mourning, faint-hearted people into colorfully dressed, faces-beaming people of joy. The world hardly recognizes us. Our presence bears witness to God and causes the world to take note of the restorative power of God.

We spent time with the prophetic words of Paul to the Thessalonians. Waiting for the Lord to come is hard, but there is work yet to do. Paul told us how to wait, what to do, what not to do, and what God is faithfully doing in the communal sanctification of a people.

Finally, we visited the most familiar prophetic figure of the New Testament, John the Baptist. In line with the prophets who came before him, he aims his light on the coming Messiah. Then he takes his place as one who bears appropriate witness by his humble posture at the feet of

Jesus. The leaders peppering John with questions lack the key Advent ingredient of the week: joy. Good news is welcomed with great joy.

As you prepare for the Fourth Sunday of Advent tomorrow, which is also the eve of our Lord's birth, may you be opened to the message that brings the deepest joy known to humankind. Rest well.

SCRIPTURE

PSALM 89:1-4, 19-26

I will sing of your steadfast love, O LORD, forever; with my mouth I will proclaim your faithfulness to all generations. I declare that your steadfast love is established forever; your faithfulness is as firm as the heavens. You said, "I have made a covenant with my chosen one; I have sworn to my servant David: 'I will establish your descendants forever and build your throne for all generations.'"

Then you spoke in a vision to your faithful one and said: "I have set the crown on one who is mighty; I have exalted one chosen from the people. I have found my servant David; with my holy oil I have anointed him; my hand shall always remain with him; my arm also shall strengthen him. The enemy shall not outwit him; the wicked shall not humble him. I will crush his foes before him and strike down those who hate him. My faithfulness and steadfast love shall be with him, and in my name his horn shall be exalted. I will set his hand on the sea and his right hand on the rivers. He shall cry to me, 'You are my Father, my God, and the Rock of my salvation!'"

—Psalm 89:1-4, 19-26

We are vulnerable, and we know it. Any serious person who thinks about the way the world is has reason to feel vulnerable. That's why we love Mary. She is a picture of vulnerability.

At the Nelson-Atkins Museum of Art in Kansas City, Missouri, you can see Mary through the eyes of different artists. In the composite, she is a mature adult who wears velvet dresses, lives in a larger-than-average home, has a chair by the window through which light cascades softly, and she likes to read. This is the Mary of classic art. She appears to be fully in charge of her space.

But we know better. Mary is an adolescent girl. She probably wears hand-me-down clothes that aren't expensive. She can't read (girls of her day rarely did). Her parents make all the decisions that affect her life, including the one that she should marry an older man named Joseph. We don't know if she even liked him. She lives in a two-bit town without a McDonald's or a stoplight.

Into the bedroom of this child comes the brightly beaming divine messenger, creating a set of contrasts that are, in my opinion, overkill. A resplendent angel versus a precocious child. A messenger of the most high God versus a girl who is barely past puberty. Holy wattage against a candlelit room. Divine might and glory against human frailty. Mary is defenseless, fragile, probably overwhelmed, and definitely vulnerable. That's why we adore her. She's like us. She has had overwhelming stuff happen to her. She has faced life with little power to make it turn out the way she wants. Forces beyond her have rearranged her life. She's the matron saint of the vulnerable. If you ever think your own story is not in the Bible, look closely at Mary. She's vulnerable, just like us.

But Mary may not be the most vulnerable one in the story. There is one who becomes even more vulnerable than she—the God who becomes dependent flesh in Mary's vulnerable womb. Christ's birth story may seem to magnify Mary, but it's really about God—and the vulnerability of God. God—the Creator—becomes creature. God—the breath of every living thing—becomes embryo. God—whose hand scoops out oceans—floats in a fetal sac. God—whose voice splits cedar trees—cries for mother's milk. God—who crushes kings' armies—can't walk. God—who feeds all living things—is hungry. God became vulnerable!

I forget that sometimes. I prefer Gabriel, frightening, powerful, mighty messenger of God. When I am vulnerable, I want to behold a delivering, transforming, world-altering, situation-changing, putting-me-back-in-control God. I ask God to meet me at the intersection of Fixed and Finished. But God has chosen to meet us in the vulnerable Christ, revealing himself at the point of our own vulnerability. Dare we meet the mighty God at the point of our own vulnerability? He's here—right here, right now. Our God has come to you on this Christmas Eve. *Where meek souls will receive him still, the dear Christ enters in.*

BLESSING

And the peace of God, which surpasses all understanding, will guard your hearts and your minds in Christ Jesus.

—Philippians 4:7

O Little Town of Bethlehem (*Sing to the Lord* #169)

O little town of Bethlehem, how still we see thee lie!
Above thy deep and dreamless sleep the silent stars go by.
Yet in thy dark streets shineth the everlasting light.
The hopes and fears of all the years are met in thee tonight.

For Christ is born of Mary; and gathered all above,
While mortals sleep, the angels keep their watch of wond'ring love.
O morning stars, together proclaim the holy birth!
And praises sing to God, the King, and peace to all on earth.

How silently, how silently the wondrous Gift is giv'n!
So God imparts to human hearts the blessings of his heav'n.
No ear may hear his coming; but in this world of sin,
Where meek souls will receive him still, the dear Christ enters in.

O holy Child of Bethlehem, descend on us, we pray.
Cast out our sin, and enter in; be born in us today.
We hear the Christmas angels, the great glad tidings tell.
O come to us, abide with us, our Lord, Emmanuel.

QUESTIONS FOR REFLECTION

1. What does vulnerability mean to you?

    ----

2. How does it change your view of God to think of God as vulnerable?

    ----

3. What does peace mean to you?

    ----

4. What can you do in your own life to bring peace?
